Department of Health

Residential
Special Schools

National Minimum Standards

Inspection Regulations

London: TSO

First published 2002

ISBN 0 11 322544 X

Web Access
This document is available on the DoH internet web site at:
http://www.doh.gov.uk/ncsc

Published by The Stationery Office and available from:

The Stationery Office
(mail, telephone, fax & e-mail orders only)
PO Box 29, Norwich, NR3 1GN
Telephone orders/General enquiries: 0870 6005522
Fax orders: 0870 6005533
E-mail: book.orders@tso.co.uk
Textphone 0870 240 3701

You can now order books online at **www.tso.co.uk**

The Stationery Office Bookshops
123 Kingsway, London, WC2B 6PQ
020 7242 6393 Fax 020 7242 6394
68-69 Bull Street, Birmingham B4 6AD
0121 236 9696 Fax 0121 236 9699
9-21 Princess Street, Manchester M60 8AS
0161 834 7201 Fax 0161 833 0634
16 Arthur Street, Belfast BT1 4GD
028 9023 8451 Fax 028 9023 5401
18-19 High Street, Cardiff CF10 1PT
029 2039 5548 Fax 029 2038 4347
71 Lothian Road, Edinburgh EH3 9AZ
0870 606 5566 Fax 0870 6065588

The Stationery Office's Accredited Agents
(see Yellow Pages)

and through good booksellers

Printed in the United Kingdom for The Stationery Office

National Minimum Standards for Residential Special Schools

A statement of national minimum standards published by the Secretary of State for Health under section 23(1) of the Care Standards Act 2000.

March 2002

National Minimum Standards for Residential Special Schools

Note

This document contains a statement of national minimum standards published by the Secretary of State under section 23(1) of the Care Standards Act 2000. The statement is applicable to special boarding schools as defined by the Education Act 1996.

The statement is accompanied, for explanatory purposes only, by an introduction to the statement as a whole, and a further introduction to each group of standards.

Each individual standard is numbered and consists of the numbered heading and numbered paragraphs. Each standard is, for explanatory purposes only, preceded by a title and an indication of the intended outcome in relation to that standard.

Department of Health

Contents

General Introduction

This document contains a statement of national minimum standards published by the Secretary of State under section 87C(1) of the Children Act 1989 as amended by the Care Standards Act 2000. The statement is applicable to residential special schools.

Each individual standard is numbered and consists of the numbered heading and numbered paragraphs. Each standard is, for explanatory purposes only, preceded by a title and an indication of the intended outcome in relation to that standard.

How the standards work

These standards are to be used by the National Care Standards Commission[1] when it takes on responsibility for the welfare inspection of boarding schools, including residential special schools, in April 2002. They are intended to safeguard and promote the welfare of children for whom accommodation is provided by a residential special school. The Secretary of State will keep the standards under review, and may publish amended standards as appropriate.

These standards are designed to be used in inspecting any school providing accommodation for any child and which is either:

(a)   a special school in accordance with sections 337 and 347(1) of the Education Act 1996; or

(b)   an independent school not falling within (a) which has as its sole or main purpose the provision of places, with the consent of the Secretary of State, for pupils with special educational needs or who are in public care,

There is a separate set of national minimum standards for all other schools which provide accommodation for children. Boarding schools which accommodate or arrange accommodation for any child for more than 295 days a year, or intend to do so, are required to register as children's homes with the National Care Standards Commission. Such schools are then subject to the Children's Homes Regulations 2001 and the national minimum standards for children's homes rather than the standards in this document.

---

1   In all references to the National Care Standards Commission inspecting schools, this should also be taken to cover inspections by any other inspector appointed by the Secretary of State, under Section 87A of the Children Act 1989, to carry out inspections of boarding schools.

The residential/care aspects are only a part (an important part) of what is a wider provision and that is essentially an educational placement that exists in order that the needs of the pupils as stated in their statements are met. The special school is firstly a school and is responsive to legislation and guidance as a school.

There are many different reasons for pupils being in residential special schools. Some are in residence because it is an essential part of their educational programme, some are in residence because of family and home difficulties and others are in residence because the provision that the school offers is geographically located too far from home for the pupils to be day attenders. Some residential schools have a number of day pupils and others have residents as a minority. These will need careful management of accommodation and relationships.

The National Care Standards Commission, or any other inspector appointed by the Secretary of State under Section 87A of the Children Act 1989 to carry out inspections of boarding schools, will assess whether the school is satisfactorily safeguarding and promoting the welfare of the children for whom accommodation is provided or arranged by reference to these standards. The Department for Education and Skills will refer where relevant to these standards, as well as the relevant Ofsted inspection framework, in any action it may take against an independent or non-maintained residential special school in relation to a failure to comply with the duty to safeguard or promote welfare. Local education authorities and the Secretary of State will also take the national minimum standards into account in any enforcement action in relation to failure to safeguard or promote the welfare of boarding pupils accommodated in any maintained residential special school. Other inspection bodies such as Ofsted and HMI also have a remit to inspect the care provision within residential special schools.

The standards are minimum standards, in the sense that they provide minimum standards below which no school is expected to fall in safeguarding and promoting the welfare of boarders. Many schools already meet these standards or exceed them.

The school will be inspected against the standards in order to determine whether it is complying with its legal obligation to safeguard and promote the welfare of boarding pupils. In carrying out its functions, the Commission's role is to consider the extent to which a school promotes and safeguards the welfare of its boarders, rather than to focus on structures and systems for their own sake. Regard will be paid to the school's admission policy and Statement of Purpose and to the views of who have chosen the school for their child.

In inspecting to these standards, the National Care Standards Commission will follow a consistent inspection methodology and reporting format across the country.

School premises

Some of the standards contained within this document, particularly around premises and accommodation of pupils, are higher than those set out in The Education (School Premises) Regulations 1999. This is due to the different nature of residential special school establishments and the particular needs of the individual children accommodated there.

Further information

These national minimum standards are the responsibility of the Secretary of State for Health, but it is the responsibility of the National Care Standards Commission to apply them to individual establishments. The Commission may be approached in the first instance regarding the application of the standards in particular circumstances. Other queries – for example about the policies behind the standards – can be addressed to the Department of Health at this e-mail address: dhmail@doh.gsi.gov.uk.

National Minimum Standards for Residential Special Schools

Statement of the school's purpose

Statement of the school's purpose

OUTCOME

Children, parents, staff and placing authorities have access to a clear statement of the school's care principles and practice for boarding pupils.

STANDARD 1

1.1 The school has a written Statement of Purpose, which accurately describes what the school sets out to do for those children it accommodates, and the manner in which care is provided. The statement can be made up of other documents, e.g., Letter of Approved Arrangements and school prospectus, which are required to include specific information.

1.2 The statement describes the overall purpose of the school and describes any theoretical or therapeutic model underpinning the practice of the school, the ethos and philosophy of the school, and an outline of any provision by the school for disabled children.

1.3 The statement, having regard to information supplied within the school prospectus, provides the name of the designated member of staff for child protection and the names and relevant professional qualifications of staff. The statement also describes:

- the range of pupil needs for which the school caters,
- its admission criteria,
- the approved number of day and residential pupils, age range and gender accommodated,
- any special religious or cultural aspects of the school,
- any special features of the school.

1.4 The statement is in a form that can be understood by placing social workers (or, where appropriate, the local education authority), staff, children, and any parent or person with parental responsibility for a child. Where it is not possible for children and/or their parents or those with parental responsibility to read the statement, the school provides, as far as possible, the information in another more suitable format such as on tape, in Braille or in a sign language, or a children's and/or parents' guide.

1.5   The range of needs to be met under the Statement of Purpose are capable of being fulfilled by the school as it currently operates, and the school only admits children whose assessed needs can be met within the purpose of the school.

1.6   The Statement of Purpose, and the policies and procedures established in accordance with it, clearly apply to both the boarding and teaching aspects of the life of a child resident at the school. The Statement, and the associated policies and procedures, do not create conflicts between 'residential' and 'day', or 'teaching' and 'care' functions of the school but identify how all those working at the school will create a continuum of care for the children.

1.8   The governing body or other proprietor (individual or organisation) carrying on the school approves the Statement of Purpose of the school, reviews and updates it at least annually, and modifies it as necessary in order to ensure that it reasonably reflects the actual current boarding and care practice at the school.

2 Children's rights

Consultation

OUTCOME

Children are encouraged and supported to make decisions about their lives and to influence the way the school is run. No child should be assumed to be unable to communicate their views.

STANDARD 2

2.1 Children's opinions, and those of their families or significant others[2], are sought over key decisions which are likely to affect their daily life and their future. Feedback is given following consultations.

2.2 Policies, which are implemented in practice, guidance and training on consulting with and involving children, their families and significant others are available to staff and supported by the school's management team.

2.3 Staff take into account the religious, racial, cultural, communication methods and linguistic backgrounds of children and their families, and know when and whom to ask for advice or assistance.

2.4 The opinions and views of children are actively sought and taken into account when decisions affecting their welfare are made. The deciding factor is what is in the child's best interest but where there is an overriding reason why a child's wishes should not be carried out the child is informed of the reasons.

2.5 The school provides frequent and suitable means for any child, using their preferred method of communication, to make their wishes and feelings known regarding their care and treatment in the school. This includes availability of different adults who understand the child's preferred method of communication.

2.6 The way the school functions does not routinely or unnecessarily diminish any child's independence or opportunity to make everyday choices.

---

2 'Significant other' refers to someone who the child or young person considers important in their lives, for example, a close friend of the family, godparent, independent advocate, teacher or partner.

2.7 Active steps are taken to enable children with any disability and/or SEN or impairment to make everyday choices and to maximise their opportunities for independence.

2.8 Each child, as far as practicable, is able to attend the services of, receive instruction in, and observe any requirement of (including dress, diet or otherwise) of their religious persuasion.

Privacy and confidentiality

OUTCOME

Children's privacy is respected and information about them is confidentially handled.

STANDARD 3

3.1 The school and staff respect a child's wishes for privacy and confidentiality so far as is consistent with good parenting and the need to protect the child.

3.2 The school provides procedural guidelines to staff on privacy and confidentiality, covering:

　i　access to case records by staff and others

　ii　passing on information with child protection implications

　iii　practical details about the way, and when, children's rooms, bathrooms and toilets are entered

　iv　showering and bathing arrangements and use of toilets

　v　personal matters such as menstruation

　vi　washing clothes

　vii　intimate personal care for disabled children, including administering medication and invasive clinical procedures where applicable.

3.3 Children's records are kept safely and securely, and the contents remain confidential and shared only with individuals with a right to access or a need to know their contents in order to safeguard and promote the child's welfare.

3.4 Staff know how to deal with and share information which they are given in confidence when necessary for child protection.

3.5 Subject to 3.6 below, children can make and receive telephone and textphone calls in private and without staff permission. Children can write and receive letters without these being read by staff and without staff permission. If children have access within the school to e-mail and/or voice mail facilities, they can send and receive messages by these media without these being read by staff. Where assistance or supervision for a child is necessary, staff enable children to use the telephone, textphone, e-mail or voice mail facilities and do not intrude on privacy where possible. Information about services (eg helplines) which children may wish to consult confidentially is available (eg displayed by the telephone) in a suitable format (e.g. Braille, large print or on tape). Children are provided with additional support to use communication aids if necessary.

3.6 Where there are clear grounds that the welfare of a child is at risk from the child's use of the telephone, textphone, through postal or electronic communications (such as a child being at risk of being procured for prostitution), staff intervene appropriately to protect the welfare of the child. Any restrictions on communication by a child placed by a placing authority must either be agreed beforehand by that authority, or, if that is not practicable, be notified without delay to the authority, and its continuation and extent be by agreement with that authority. For a child placed by a parent, the school agrees the continuation and extent of any restriction with that parent. Any such agreement must be recorded in writing and placed in the child's file.

3.7 The school provides space for children to meet privately with parents and others.

3.8 Staff are sensitive to gender issues especially when dealing with children of the opposite sex.

3.9 Staff supervision of children does not intrude inappropriately or in a way that unnecessarily embarrasses children.

3.10 Where the children at the school require staff help with intimate care or bodily functions, all staff involved have received appropriate training and are provided with clear and appropriate written guidelines on provision of such assistance, which are followed in practice. These guidelines cover boundaries to be observed (including provision of such care to children of the opposite sex) and the requirement for the child concerned, where practicable, to be enabled to express choices and to give consent regarding provision of their intimate care. Staff involved have also received any necessary training in the use of any equipment involved in caring for the child (eg lifts or hoists), and are competent in their safe operation with the child concerned.

3.11 The school provides guidance, available to staff and children, on when it may be necessary to search a child's possessions. Children's belongings are searched only in accordance with the guidance, and only on clear grounds, which are explained to the child concerned, and where failure to carry out the search might put at risk the welfare of the child or others. All such searches are documented, showing the time and date and the reason for the search, noting what if anything was found, who carried out the search and who was present at the time which, where possible, will include the child. Such records should be signed by all those present including, where possible, the child.

Complaints and representation procedures

OUTCOME

Children's complaints are addressed without delay and children are kept informed of progress in their consideration.

STANDARD 4

4.1 **Children know how and feel able to complain if they are unhappy with any aspect of living in the school, and feel confident that any complaint is addressed seriously and without delay[3].**

4.2 Children, and where appropriate their families, significant others and independent visitors, are provided with information on how to complain, including how they can secure access to an independent advocate and when such a person is next visiting the establishment, where known.

4.3 The school has a written policy and procedural guidelines on considering and responding to representations and complaints in accordance with legal requirements and relevant government guidance. The policy clearly explains the right and the means for children to access the complaints procedure of their placing authority where they are placed by such an authority.

The school's complaints procedure:

- enables children, staff, family members and others involved with children of the school outside the school, to make both minor and major complaints
- precludes any person who is the subject of a formal complaint from taking any responsibility for the consideration or response to that complaint
- expressly forbids any reprisals against children or others making a complaint
- includes provision for both informal attempts, such as negotiation, arbitration and mediation, at resolving the complaint and for the child and any complainant to have the matter pursued further if not satisfied with the proposed informal resolution
- provides appropriately for the handling of any complaint made against the Head of the school
- requires a written record to be made and kept of:
  - the person making the complaint
  - the date of the complaint
  - the nature of the complaint
  - any action taken, and
  - the outcome of the complaint.

---

3   In maintained schools, governing bodies have a legal duty to establish and publish a complaints procedure (s39.1 of The School Standards and Framework Act 1998). (In independent schools there is no such legal requirement though this may change if the current Education Bill is enacted)

- does not restrict the issues complained about

- provides for relevant issues to be referred promptly elsewhere, including to the local social services authority where child protection issues are involved

- is accessible to disabled children and in a suitable form for children with learning needs and in a manner which suits a child's preferred method of communication

- provides, where possible, for children to take complaints to a person outside the school (who may be a counsellor), such a person having been checked through the same staff recruitment checks as are required for school staff, to provide an independent element in the procedure for complaints children consider to be serious.

- enables people other than the child to make complaints on behalf of the child, provided the child consents to this

- details how external complaints about the children will be managed (e.g. those from local shop keepers, neighbours, the police etc).

4.4 Staff receive training in the complaints procedures covering the following areas:

- what constitutes a complaint

- what the procedure is for dealing with an informal complaint in the school and how this is recorded

- to whom a complaint is made outside the school

- the procedure to be followed should a complaint not be resolved promptly by informal means, including who should be notified and the keeping of records

- how the child can be assisted in making a complaint.

4.5 The school provides the complainant with details of the outcome of their complaint in an accessible format at the earliest opportunity. The complainant is kept informed of the progress on their complaint.

4.6 The Head of the school or a designated member of the senior management team regularly reviews the records of complaints by children or concerning the welfare of children, to check satisfactory operation of the complaints procedure, and to identify both patterns of complaint and action taken on individual complaints. The Head or designated person takes any appropriate action from such review in relation to the school's policies and practices, as well as taking any necessary further follow up action in relation to individual cases.

4.7 Serious complaints against the school or the staff of the school are notified to the National Care Standards Commission This is in addition to any other notification requirements placed on the school by a Local Education Authority, the Department for Education and Skills or other official body.

4.8 Children and their parents are told how they can make a complaint directly to the National Care Standards Commission).

4.9 Any recent complaints have been resolved either to the complainant's satisfaction, or with an otherwise satisfactory outcome.

3

Child protection

Procedures and training

OUTCOME

The welfare of children is promoted, children are protected from abuse, and an appropriate response is made to any allegation or suspicion of abuse.

STANDARD 5

5.1 **There are systems in place in the school which aim to prevent abuse of children and suspicions or allegations of abuse are properly responded to. Theses are known and understood by all staff (including ancillary, volunteer and agency staff).**

5.2 A copy of the local Area Child Protection Committee (ACPC) procedures, where available from the ACPC, is kept in the school. The Head or designated person for child protection has read these, understands them and is knowledgeable about them.

5.3 The school's child protection procedures are consistent with the local policies and procedures agreed by the Area Child Protection Committee (ACPC) relevant to the geographical area in which the school is situated. The school's child protection procedures have been submitted for consideration and comment to the local ACPC and, where appropriate, to the Local Education Authority and any comments taken into account in revising the school's procedures.

5.4 The school's procedures for responding to allegations or suspicions of abuse to a child (by a member of staff, another child, a visitor, a member of the child's family, at school, or elsewhere outside the school) include all the requirements set out at Appendix 1.

5.5 The school's policies and procedures and its induction process for staff make it clear that failure by a member of staff to report actual or reasonably suspected physical, sexual or emotional abuse or neglect of a child is a disciplinary offence.

5.6 The school has written guidance for staff who are subject to allegations against them. Such guidance will make clear ways in which staff may have access to information and support whilst an investigation ensues.

5.7 Written procedural guidance for staff is in line with ACPC guidance and procedures and clearly demonstrates the systems the school requires in order to protect children and minimise the risk of abuse whilst the child is living in the school. Such guidance must include the procedure for dealing with out of authority placements.

5.8 The Head of the school ensures there is training for all staff, including ancillary staff, agency staff and volunteers, in the prevention and recognition of abuse, dealing with disclosures or suspicions of abuse, and the school's child protection procedures. This training is included in induction programmes for new staff, including temporary staff, and is ongoing for the staff group in keeping with the aims and objectives of the school.

5.9 The school and staff have routine links with other agencies concerned with child protection e.g. placing authorities, schools, hospitals, general practitioners, etc., and do not work in isolation from them.

5.10 The school follows any local interagency protocols on prevention and investigation of child prostitution.

Anti-bullying

OUTCOME

Children are protected from bullying by others.

STANDARD 6

6.1 The school has, and follows, an anti-bullying policy, with which children and staff are familiar and which is effective in practice. Where possible children in the school contribute to the development of the policy.

6.2 The school has an anti-bullying policy which includes:

- a definition of bullying which extends to, name calling, being 'picked on' and the use of prejudicial remarks or actions, which is reviewed frequently with staff and children, and which includes bullying by staff, by children and by visitors and bullying that may occur elsewhere than in the school
- measures to prevent bullying and to respond to observed or reported bullying
- training for staff in awareness of, and effective strategies to counter bullying.

6.3 This policy is available and known to both staff and children, including agency, temporary and recently appointed staff.

6.4 Children who are bullied are supported, and children who may bully others are also given suitable guidance.

6.5 The school regularly carries out recorded risk assessments of the times, places and circumstances in which the risk of bullying including bullying amounting to abuse by other pupils is greatest, and takes resultant action where feasible to reduce or counteract the risk of bullying.

Notifications

OUTCOME

All significant events relating to the protection of children in the school are notified by the Head of the school or designated person to the appropriate authorities.

STANDARD 7

7.1 **All significant events relating to the protection of children in the school are notified by the Head of the school or designated person to the appropriate authorities.**

7.2 The school has a system in place to notify promptly the National Care Standards Commission, the local social services authority, the Department for Education and Skills, the placing authority and, for maintained schools, the responsible local education authority of the following events:

- the death of a child whilst at, or immediately following, being at the school, and such details of the circumstances that are known
- inappropriate conduct by a staff member such that he/she might not be a suitable person for work involving children
- suffering of serious harm by a child at the school or during school arranged activities. This would include where an allegation has been made which indicates that abuse of a child may have occurred
- any serious illness or accident involving a child at the school
- the outbreak in the school of any notifiable infectious disease.

7.3 The school has a system in place to make the required notification under the Protection of Children Act of any dismissal or resignation of a member of staff or other person working at the school, in circumstances which suggest their unsuitability to work with children.

7.4 A written record has been kept which includes details of the action taken, and the outcome of any action or investigation, following any of the above notifiable events that have occurred since the previous inspection.

7.5 The school has a system for notification to the authorities and individuals, of any serious concerns about the emotional or mental health of a child such that a mental health assessment would be requested under the Mental Health Act 1983.

7.6 The school has a system in place for notifying the National Care Standards Commission, of any serious incident within the school which has necessitated the police being called to the school, whether or not injury has been caused to a child. This is additional to any requirements for maintained schools to report such matters to the local education authority.

7.7 Staff in the school promptly notify the child's parent, and where applicable the child's placing authority, of any serious incidents involving their child, including any allegation that the child has committed an offence.

Absence of a child without authority

OUTCOME

Children who are absent without authority are protected in accordance with written guidance and responded to positively on return.

STANDARD 8

8.1 The school takes steps to ensure that children who are absent from the school without consent are protected in line with written policy and guidance.

8.2 The school has written procedures identifying action to be taken when a child is absent without authority, which are known to staff, children and their parents.

8.3 The school's procedures cover the following:
- searching for any child missing or believed to have run away from the school
- reporting children that have been missing for 3 hours or more to the police, to the child's parents (if appropriate), to the child's placing authority (if any) and, if a maintained school, to the appropriate local education authority.
- action to obtain information about the whereabouts of a missing child and to try to ensure the safety and welfare of that child
- the collection and return of missing children when found
- action to be taken on the child's return.

8.4 On return to the school, the child is seen wherever possible (and if s/he wishes it) by a person charged with his/her pastoral care, to consider the reasons for the absence without authority. Where this does not happen it should be recorded and agreed with the placing authority (if any) or the child's parents, if appropriate. Any reasons given are considered in relation to how the child is cared for and the school's care practice.

8.5 Any report from a child that s/he went missing because of abuse at the school is referred immediately to the local social services department for consideration under Area Child Protection procedures, and appropriate action is taken by the school to protect the child concerned and other children as necessary.

8.6 Written records are made of the circumstances of all incidents of absence without authority, all action taken by staff, the circumstances of the child's return, any reasons given by the child for going missing, and any action taken in the light of those reasons.

8.7 All staff are aware of, and do not exceed, the measures they may properly take to prevent a child leaving without permission under current legislation and government guidance.[4]

8.8 A system is in place for monitoring children's absences from the school without authority. Where a high level or worrying pattern of absences is recorded, the school initiates both a review of the care plan of any individual child involved, and of the relevant current care practice of the school.

8.9 When a child has run away in the past and is at risk of doing so again if not supervised, the school has procedures to monitor the child and to specify how the child may be prevented from leaving the school without authority in the future. Procedures may include physical modification to the premises, behavioural and/or therapeutic approaches to change the child's behaviour, or physical restraint (in accordance with agreed guidance on physical restraint). Any such measures must be used as agreed in the child's care plan.

---

4 (s.5 50(a) Education Act 1996). DfES circular 10/98.

4

Care and control

Relationship with children

OUTCOME

Children have sound relationships with staff based on honesty and mutual respect.

STANDARD 9

9.1 **Relationships between staff and children are based on mutual respect and understanding and clear professional and personal boundaries which are effective for both the individuals and the group.**

9.2 Staff employed at the school are able to set and maintain safe, consistent and understandable boundaries for the children in relation to acceptable behaviour.

9.3 Expectations of behaviour for both staff and children are clearly understood and negotiated by those living and working at the school, including exercising appropriate control over children in the interests of their own welfare and the protection of others.

9.4 In day to day decision making, staff demonstrate an appropriate balance between:

- each child's wishes and preferences,
- the needs of individual children,
- the needs of the group of children resident at the time, and
- the protection of themselves, other staff, children and others (including the public) from harm.

9.5 All staff in direct contact with children receive training in positive care and control of children including praising children for their achievements.

9.6 Children in the school are looked after without favouritism or antipathy towards any individual or group within the school.

9.7 Communication between staff and children in the school is generally positive, and disagreements between children and staff are dealt with reasonably.

9.8 The deployment of staff facilitates continuity of staff providing care to individual children, and maximises children's choices of which staff members provide their personal care, where appropriate. The school can demonstrate that, as far as is possible, children are able to choose who provides their personal care.

Measures of control, discipline and physical intervention

OUTCOME

Children are assisted to develop appropriate behaviour through the encouragement of acceptable behaviour and constructive staff responses to inappropriate behaviour.

STANDARD 10

10.1 **Staff respond positively to acceptable behaviour, and where the behaviour of children is regarded as unacceptable by staff, it is responded to by constructive disciplinary measures which are approved by the Head of care.**

10.2 The school has a clear and appropriate written policy and procedures on the control, disciplinary and physical intervention measures which may be used at the school, which also emphasises the need to positively reinforce children for the achievement of acceptable behaviour.

10.3 Any individual boarding house or unit disciplinary policy or practice is both consistent with overall school policy, and formally sanctioned by the school.

10.4 Measures of control and sanctions are based on establishing positive relationships with children and are designed to help the child. Such measures are fair and consistently applied; they also encourage reparation and restitution and reduce the likelihood of negative behaviour becoming a focus of attention.

10.5 Any measures taken to respond to unacceptable behaviour are appropriate to the age, understanding and individual needs of the child, for example taking into account that unacceptable or challenging behaviour may be the result of illness, bullying, certain disabilities such as autism, or communication difficulties. Specific measures of control or physical intervention are selected, avoided or adapted as necessary to take the child's needs, characteristics plus any disability/SEN into account.

10.6 No unreasonable, idiosyncratic or excessive sanctions are used by staff or others at the school, including any sanction intended to cause pain, anxiety or humiliation, nor are any of the following used as a punishment:

- corporal punishment,
- any form of hitting of a child (including hitting a child in anger or retaliation),
- deprivation of access to food or drink,
- enforced eating or drinking,
- prevention of contact by telephone or letter with parents or any appropriate independent listener or helpline,
- requirement to wear distinctive clothing or the wearing of nightclothes by day,
- use or withholding of medical or dental treatment,

- intentional deprivation of sleep,
- use of fines other than by way of reparation and not exceeding two thirds of the child's immediately available pocket money provision,
- locking in a room or area of a building,
- intimate physical examination of the child,
- withholding of any aids or equipment needed by a child.

10.7 Sanctions applied to groups of children are not used as punishment for the offences of individual children or as a means of applying group pressure against a child.

10.8 Children, including prefects and those in other positions of authority, are not given authority to use any sanctions or physical intervention against other children.

10.9 A record of all sanctions applied is kept in a bound and numbered book which contains a list of permitted sanctions. The record is made within 24 hours and legibly recorded. Each entry includes:

- the name of the child,
- the date and location of the incident which lead to the sanction being applied,
- details of the inappropriate behaviour,
- the nature of the sanction,
- the name of the staff member giving the sanction,
- the name(s) of any other staff present,
- the effectiveness and any consequences of the sanction,
- the signature of the staff member concerned.

Where sanctions are imposed, children are encouraged to write or otherwise have their views recorded and sign their names against them, if possible, in the records kept by the school.

10.10 Physical intervention is normally only used to prevent likely injury to the child concerned or to others, or likely serious damage to property. Physical intervention is not used as a punishment, as a means to enforce compliance with instructions, or in response to challenging behaviour other than in situations set out in s550A of the Education Act 1996.

10.11 The school has a stated policy on the use of physical intervention and the circumstances in which it may be used, which is consistent with any relevant current government guidance on approved methods of physical intervention and is appropriate to the needs and difficulties of the children at the school. All staff of the school are aware of, and follow in practice, the school's policy on use and techniques of physical intervention.

10.12 The school provides or secures the provision of training for staff in safe and appropriate physical intervention techniques with children, and the circumstances in which they may be used, which includes training in reducing or avoiding the need to use physical intervention.

10.13   Physical interventions are not excessive or unreasonable.

10.14   A record of any use of physical intervention on a child by an adult is kept in a separate bound and numbered book, and includes:

- the name of the child,
- the date and location where the physical intervention took place,
- details of the behaviour requiring use of physical intervention,
- the nature of the physical intervention used,
- the duration of the physical intervention,
- the name of the staff member(s) using physical intervention, the name(s) of any other staff present,
- the effectiveness and any consequences of the physical intervention,
- any injuries caused to or reported by the child or any other person, and
- the signature of the Head, the head of care or a person authorised by the Head,
- the governors or owners of the school.

Such records to be completed at the earliest opportunity and no later than 24 hours after the incident. Where physical interventions are used children are encouraged to write or otherwise have their views recorded and sign their names against them, if possible, in the records kept by the school.

10.15   The school's records of sanctions and physical intervention are reviewed at least twice a term by a senior member of the school's staff to monitor compliance with the school's disciplinary, control and physical intervention procedures and to identify any patterns in incidents leading to sanctions or physical intervention action becoming necessary.

10.16   The Head reviews both the care of individual children and the school's current care practice in the light of the recorded incidence and pattern of incidents requiring sanctions or physical intervention. The Head records any comment on the appropriateness of individual uses of sanctions or physical intervention, together with any subsequent action taken.

10.17   Records of serious sanctions or physical intervention on a child are also made on the individual child's file (to which a parent or placing authority has access).

10.18   A representative of the school's governing body, proprietor or the person carrying on the school, reads and makes written comment upon the use of sanctions and physical intervention during visits to the school made under Standard 33.

10.19   All staff who have direct contact with children have read, show an understanding of and have signed a copy of the school's policies on measures of control, discipline and physical intervention, and evidence of this is retained on their personnel file. The policy details how staff are to be debriefed following any physical intervention.

10.20   Information is appropriately given to all children about the expectations of behaviour at the school, any rules they are expected to keep to, and what sanctions and physical interventions are used and how they relate to unacceptable conduct. This information is also made available to parents and placing authorities as appropriate.

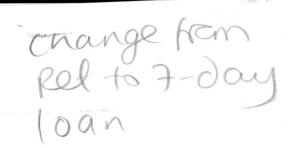
change from
Ref to 7-day
loan

⟶) develop a proper awareness of their rights and

dren alike are clear that each individual has rights and

hose who live in the school, those who work there and

nity to discuss incidents and express their views either

m or a house or unit meeting where unsafe behaviour

d adults.

guidance on police involvement in the school, which

sible with the local police and which staff are

control. Staff agree practicable and acceptable means

l control problems of both groups of children and

f their histories, any current problems and the care

cal authorities.

10.25   Standards of behaviour at the school and in the community are satisfactory, having regard to the needs of the children.

10.26   The school's disciplinary policy includes a clear statement of the circumstances and manner in which a child may be excluded from school. Exclusions are only used for serious offences and are applied fairly. Exclusions do not transfer the child to circumstances which the school has reason to believe may put the child's welfare at risk. The disciplinary policy includes details of the appeals procedure and makes this known to the child and to the parents (where appropriate), any independent advocate representing the child and the placing authority.

5 Quality of care

Admission and leaving

OUTCOME
Children experience planned and sensitively handled admission and leaving processes.

STANDARD 11

11.1 Admission and leaving processes are planned and agreed with the child – and, as appropriate, with parents and carers and placing authorities – as far as possible and handled with sensitivity and care by those concerned.

11.2 There are procedures for introducing children on admission

- to the school, the staff and the children living there,
- to the school's daily routine and procedures, and
- to the school's expectations of the child and what s/he can expect of staff.

These procedures include

- the provision of information about the school in a suitable form to the child,
- personal guidance and support following admission,
- review of how the child is settling following admission to the school, and
- with appropriate action to assist settling where indicated.

11.3 The school makes reasonable efforts to obtain all necessary information about a child prior to (or in an emergency, at the time of) admission. This information includes:

- whether the child is in care and if so the name of a contact person in the child's placing authority,
- any current care plan relating to the child,
- the name and means of contacting the child's parents or legal guardians,
- any current health, educational or personal care needs of the child,
- any matters which may make the child particularly vulnerable or a danger to others, and
- where appropriate, details of the child's preferred method of communication.

11.4 A review meeting is initiated as soon as possible (and never longer than four school weeks) after any emergency admission to consider whether the child admitted in emergency should remain at the school, or whether it is in that child's interests to move to a different placement. Such a review meeting to include, so far as is possible, at least one representative of each of the following:

- the school,

- the placing authority (where applicable)

- the parents or those with parental responsibility

- those with significant involvement with the child (such as social services or health services) and, where possible, the child.

11.5 Both the needs of the child concerned, and the likely effects of his/her admission upon the existing group of children, are taken into account in decisions on admission to the school. Where Heads do not control their own admissions they must inform their local education authority or the body controlling admissions of their reservations about any admission, in writing, and maintain a copy of that notification at the school.

11.6 Where children are to leave the school on a planned date, children are prepared for leaving the school well in advance of the planned date of departure, and are given appropriate information and guidance to assist in the process of transition.

Residential contribution to education

OUTCOME

The school's residential provision actively supports children's educational progress at the school.

STANDARD 12

12.1 Care staff and the school's residential provision and activities actively contribute to individual children's educational progress, and care staff actively support children's education, ensuring regular attendance, punctuality and a minimum of interruption during the school day.

12.2 Care staff are familiar with the educational needs and progress of the children in their care, and they inform teaching staff of any information which will assist in supporting the child in school time. They contribute to the annual review of the statement and participate where necessary in the implementation of the individual educational plan.

12.3 Children are provided with facilities in residential units that are conducive to study and doing any homework, and are actively encouraged and supported by residential and care staff in doing so.

12.4 Children have access to books and other educational aids (that are appropriate for their age and the stage of their educational needs) to assist with their education outside class time.

12.5 Where appropriate the school provides children with access to library facilities suitable to their needs and interests, for both educational and recreational reading.

12.6 Residential, care and teaching staff work together to identify means of encouraging each child's personal, social and educational development and achievement, and contribute consistently to encouraging development in their work with the child.

12.7 Where appropriate, children are assisted by teaching and care staff in their preparation for independent living.

Leisure and activities

OUTCOME

Children have ample opportunity to engage in purposeful and enjoyable activities both within the school and in the local community.

STANDARD 13

13.1 Children have ample opportunity to engage in purposeful and enjoyable activities both within the school and in the local community.

13.2 The school provides a range and choice of activities for boarding pupils outside class time, both indoors and outdoors and including appropriate trips, throughout the year.

13.3 Children are encouraged and given opportunities to take part in activities which take account of their race, culture, language, religion, interests, abilities and disabilities. Birthdays, name days, cultural and religious festivals are celebrated (where appropriate) and children participate with staff in planning these events together.

13.4 Children have an appropriate balance between free time and organised activities during the evenings and weekends.

13.5 There are significant activities for pupils at weekends, or at other times when the number of pupils remaining at school outside class time may be reduced.

13.6 Supervised and unsupervised activities take into account the safety of children at all times and where high or unusual hazards are involved, a recorded risk assessment is made and any indicated action is taken to minimise unnecessary risks. Any high risk activity provided or arranged for children is supervised by persons holding the relevant qualification to supervise children's involvement in the activity concerned (such as the qualification for instructing or supervising children awarded by the recognised national body for the activity concerned). Appropriate and well maintained safety equipment is used. Satisfactory support is available, and given, to all children in order that they can communicate their wishes.

13.7 Staff in the school take steps to engage children in purposeful activities suitable to their age, interests, talents, abilities and any disability and/or SEN. Children's views are regularly sought and taken into account by staff in the selection and planning of activities. Support is available to enable disabled children to enjoy a range of activities within and outside the school.

13.8 Children have access to and a choice in the selection of newspapers, books, magazines and comics subject to their suitability. Children's age, gender, culture and interests are catered for. Children have access to suitable toys, music, books and games.

13.9 Consideration is given to individual circumstances of children in watching videos and television, and in using computer games and accessing the internet. Videos, games consoles and other computer games may only be watched/played by children of the intended age range. No school shall have any videos or games certified as only suitable for over 18's in areas where they could be accessed by those under 18. Systems and policies are in place to safeguard children when computer networking or on the internet and also to prevent excessive use of the television and computers.

Health and intimate care

OUTCOME

Children live in a healthy environment and the health and intimate care needs of each child are identified and promoted.

STANDARD 14

14.1 The school actively promotes the health care of each child and meets any intimate care needs.

14.2 The physical, emotional and mental health needs of each child are identified and actively promoted in the day to day care of the child. The school provides children with guidance, advice and support on health and personal care issues appropriate to the needs and wishes of each child.

14.3 Children with particular health problems (including asthma, bedwetting, sickle cell anaemia or diabetes) or a disability including physical or sensory impairment or learning needs, are provided with appropriate support and help to avoid potential embarrassment and negative reactions by others. The school implements any treatment, within the capabilities of the staff, which is prescribed or included in a child's care plan, taking the child's wishes into account.

14.4 The school has a policy and written guidance, implemented in practice, on promoting the health of children in the school. The school also provides guidance, advice and support, appropriate to the child's age, needs, culture and wishes, in relation to health and social issues. Where possible, children are given opportunities to discuss these issues openly and honestly with staff and their peers. Requirements under this standard include:

- nutrition and diet

- exercise and rest

- personal hygiene

- sexual education and health

- the effects of alcohol, smoking, solvents and other substances

- HIV and AIDS and other blood borne diseases

- Protecting oneself from prejudice, bullying and abuse.

14.5 The school has satisfactory arrangements for each child to receive medical, optical and dental treatment while accommodated at school.

14.6 Each child has a clear written health plan or similar document covering:

- medical history

- any necessary preventive measures

- allergies or known adverse reactions to medication

- dental health needs

- hearing needs

- optical needs

- records of developmental checks

- specific treatment therapies or remedial programmes needed in relation to physical, emotional or mental health

- health monitoring required of staff

- intimate care or bodily functions requiring staff help

- the involvement of a child's parents or significant others in health issues.

14.7 Issues of personal hygiene are dealt with sensitively.

14.8 The needs of refugee children, asylum seekers and children from different racial and cultural backgrounds are understood by staff and specialist advice is sought when necessary.

14.9 Staff are trained in the use of First Aid and first aid boxes are provided within the school. At least one staff member on each shift and in each building where children sleep, holds a current first aid qualification.

14.10 The school has effective arrangements to secure specialist medical services including psychological and psychiatric advice, treatment and support to children needing these services. The school has obtained, and retains on file for each child, prior written permission from a person or body with parental responsibility for that child, for the administration of first aid and appropriate non-prescription medication and to seek medical, optical or dental treatment when required.

14.11   If the school employs a person to work as a nurse at the school, that staff member holds a current registration as a nurse, and the school has confirmed on appointment that they are registered with the United Kingdom Central Council [or when in operation the Nursing and Midwifery Council]. The title of 'nurse' is not used for staff not so registered. If the school employs a person as a nurse, that nurse should have access to a named senior nurse or doctor for professional guidance and consultation.

14.12   Children, subject to their age and understanding, can choose whether or not they are accompanied by a member of staff – ideally of either sex/gender of that staff member - when being seen by a doctor, nurse or dentist, and, as far as practicable, to see a doctor of either gender if they wish. Where possible appropriate staff support or an independent person is made available by the school to allow a child to communicate effectively with health professionals.

14.13   Children competent to do so are enabled to make choices concerning their nursing, medical or dental treatment.

14.14   First aid and minor illness treatment are given at the school by competent designated staff (eg by or under the supervision of a qualified first aider or, where the school has one, a nurse).

14.15   Prescribed medication is only given to the child for whom it was prescribed, in accordance with the prescription or instructions from the pharmacy, and is not kept for general use for other people (children or staff) or added to 'stock' for such use.

14.16   Prescribed and 'household' medication, other than that kept by individual children keeping their own medication, is kept securely (eg in a locked cabinet and in a labelled container). Instructions for usage are kept with the medication.

14.17   There is a policy and written guidance, implemented in practice for administering and storing medication.

14.18   The school has secured, and follows, qualified medical, pharmaceutical or nursing advice in a written protocol on the provision of non-prescription 'household' medicines to children.

14.19   Children keeping and administering their own medication are assessed by staff as sufficiently responsible to do so, and are able to store their medication somewhere not readily accessible to other children.

14.20   A written record is kept by the school of all medication, treatment and first aid given to children, giving name, date, medication/treatment, reason for administration (if not prescribed), which is signed by the responsible member of staff and is regularly monitored by an appropriate designated senior member of staff.

14.21   Children are given medication as prescribed for them, any refusal to take medication is recorded and if frequent, reported to the prescribing practitioner.

14.22   A written record is kept of all significant illnesses, accidents or injuries to children during their placement at the school.

14.23   Where school staff carry out medical or nursing procedures for a disabled child (eg catheter care, administration of oxygen, administration of rectal diazepam, management of prostheses), these are only carried out on the written authorisation of the prescribing doctor or the responsible nurse in relation to the individual child concerned, and by staff authorised and trained to do so. Records are kept of all such tasks carried out.

14.24   Where children are isolated and in bed due to sickness they have appropriate methods of summoning adult assistance and are checked regularly.

14.25   Subject to medical confidentiality, and any other legal restrictions, the school informs parents about their children's health problems and treatment.

Provision and preparation of meals

OUTCOME

Children are provided with healthy, nutritious meals that meet their dietary needs.

STANDARD 15

15.1   Children are provided with adequate quantities of suitably prepared wholesome and nutritious food, having regard to their needs and wishes, and have the opportunity to learn to prepare their own meals. Where appropriate special dietary needs due to health, religious persuasion, racial origin or cultural background are met, including the choice of a vegetarian meal for children who wish it.

15.2   Where possible meals are set up to be well-managed, orderly, social occasions.

15.3   Subject to dietary needs, children have a choice of main course at each main meal. Children are consulted over the planning of menus and encouraged to state their preferences for food and drink which are taken into account wherever possible.

15.4   A record of menus (as served) is kept in the school for one year and available to inspectors. Menus are not repeated on a weekly or more frequent cycle.

15.5   The local Environmental Health Service has assessed the storage and preparation provision of the school and any recommendations are implemented within the timescale advised.

15.6   Medical advice is sought if children consistently refuse to eat and for those who over eat or have other eating disorders.

15.7   Children are not routinely excluded from communal meals.

15.8   Dining rooms and their furnishings are suitable for the numbers and needs of children and staff dining in them.

15.9   Crockery and cutlery and any special feeding apparatus are sufficient and clean, and suitable for any children with physical disabilities requiring special cutlery.

15.10   Where practicable and with such assistance as they may require, children are able to prepare snacks and drinks for themselves at reasonable times, and have opportunities to gain experience in the preparation and cooking of food, receiving appropriate support in those tasks and using a kitchen suitable for their use.

15.11   Staff involved in preparing food for others receive relevant briefing or training in safe food handling and hygiene.

15.12   The school provides meals, with drinks, at reasonable set mealtimes. At other reasonable times food is either provided or readily available to children when they miss a set mealtime.

15.13   Drinking water is readily available to children, unless this is not appropriate, in the school at all reasonable times.

15.14   Any meals served to children away from the dining table/area meet the same standards as those served in the dining area.

15.15   Any assistance needed in eating by children with disabilities is provided as and when required in an appropriate manner, which promotes dignity and choice.

Personal appearance, clothing, requisites and personal money

OUTCOME

Children can wear their own clothing outside school time, can secure personal requisites and stationery while at school, and are helped to look after their own money.

STANDARD 16

16.1   Children are provided for adequately on an individual basis and encouraged to exercise their own preferences in the choice of clothing and personal requisites. Children who require assistance to choose what they wear and/or how they spend their money are provided with the assistance they need in a way which maximises their choices.

16.2   Children are able to bring their own clothing to school, to store this at school, and to wear their own reasonable choice of clothing outside class time.

16.3   Where possible, children are able to purchase personal requisites and stationery, either at school or from a nearby shop.

16.4   Children are able to keep their clothing and personal requisites and toiletries for their own exclusive use.

16.5   Young women have their own supply of sanitary protection and do not have to request it from a central stock.

16.6   Staff provide guidance as needed to children on the use of toiletries and sanitary protection.

16.7   Where appropriate children's money is held in safe keeping for them and, wherever possible, children sign the records. They are encouraged and assisted to manage and budget their own money.

6

Planning for care

Care planning and placement plan

OUTCOME

Children have their needs assessed and written plans outline how these needs will be met while at school.

STANDARD 17

Note: Standards 17.1, 17.2 and 17.5 are requirements only where schools do not otherwise hold this information in the child's statement of special educational need and/or care plan. Where such information is held in one or other of those documents they can be substituted for 'placement plan' throughout these standards. Where only part of the information is held the remainder must be collated and attached to either the care plan or the statement of special educational need.

17.1 There is a written placement plan specifying how the school will care for each boarding pupil in accordance with his or her assessed needs, the school cares for that child in accordance with that plan, monitors progress in relation to that plan, and updates that plan as necessary.

17.2 The school produces a written placement plan, agreed as far as is practicable with the child, the child's parents and any placing authority for the child. It identifies the needs of that child that the school will aim to meet and specifying how the school will care for the child and promote their welfare on a day to day basis. Similar consultation occurs where significant changes are made to the placement plan. The plan is consistent with the care plan of the placing authority for any child placed by such a local authority. The placement plan is regularly reviewed and amended as necessary to reflect significant changes in the child's needs or progress in his or her development.

17.3 Each child has at least one key worker (or similar person) within the school who provides individual guidance and support to the child. They regularly make time available to the child to enable the child to seek guidance, advice and support on any matter. They monitor that the school is complying on a day to day basis with the child's placement plan.

17.4 The child's wishes are sought and taken into account in the selection of their key worker/s and their wishes taken into account if they request a change of key worker.

17.5 The school's placement plan includes:

- health needs and health promotion
- method/s of communication and how they will be met
- contributing to education needs and attainment targets
- cultural, religious, language and racial needs and how they will be met
- leisure needs
- contact arrangements with family, friends and significant others
- managing and working with any disabilities or behavioural difficulties the child has
- clear instructions on the administration of any medication or other routine or emergency treatment while the child is at school (any necessary medical prescriptions, authorisations and staff training being secured before the child's admission)
- provision of intimate care to the child where required.

17.6 Support for disabled children appropriate to meet their methods of communication is provided to help them become active in making decisions about their lives.

17.7 Where feasible children in the school know the content of their placement plans, and confirm that the school is providing care for them that is consistent with these.

17.8 The school contributes appropriately to all statutory reviews for children, enables, as far as possible, children to contribute to and understand any processes of review that apply to them, and actively implements actions agreed for the school to implement following statutory reviews.

Children's individual case files

OUTCOME

Children's needs, development and progress is recorded to reflect their individuality and their group interactions.

STANDARD 18

18.1 Each child has permanent private and secure records of their history and progress, which can, in compliance with legal requirements for safeguards, be seen by the child.

18.2 A child's file/s contains the following information:

- name, gender and date of birth
- religious persuasion (if any)
- described racial origin, cultural and linguistic background
- home address

- name, address and telephone number for emergency contact with parents and for each person with parental responsibility

- the name and contact details for the person or authority responsible for the placement of the child at the school

- whether the child is in care and details of any known court orders affecting his or her care

- dates and details of any unauthorised absences from the school

- The date of, and reason for, any visit to the child whilst in the school

- The date and circumstances of any measure of control, restraint or discipline used on the child

- a copy of any statement of special educational needs maintained in relation to the child under section 324 of the Education Act 1996, with details of any such needs.

- special dietary, health and dental needs, if any

- contact arrangements, and any restrictions on contact or communication, with parents and others

- current and past placement or other plans

- the name and address of the general practitioner with whom the child is registered, and of the child's registered dental practitioner

- details of any accidents, injuries or serious illnesses of the child while accommodated by the school

- immunisations, allergies, medical, health or developmental tests or examinations carried out while accommodated by the school

- medication (both prescribed and non-prescription) given to the child by staff of the school and medication controlled by the child themselves

- deposit or withdrawal of money or valuables for safekeeping by the school, with dates and details.

18.3   Written entries on the child's file/s are signed and dated and the name of the signatory clearly identified.

18.4   Children are made aware that they may read their files if they wish, confidential or third party information excepted, and add personal statements or statements correcting errors.

18.5   Any individual pupil records kept by the school are kept for at least 21 years from the date of birth of the child or passed to the next school and a receipt obtained.

General school records

OUTCOME

There are adequate records of both the staff and child groups of the school.

STANDARD 19

19.1 **The school maintains clear and accurate records on the staff and child groups of the school, and major events affecting the school and children resident there.**

19.2 The school keeps all the following records, and keeps them up to date:

- for each child resident in the school, a register showing:
  - the dates of admission and departure of each child
  - who was responsible for their placement in the school
  - where they were living/accommodated prior to arriving at the school
  - where they are living/accommodated on leaving the school, and
  - the placing authority and legal status (if applicable)
- for all staff and other persons working at the school (including agency staff and volunteers), an employees' register showing:
  - the full name, gender, address and date of birth
  - relevant qualifications and experience for working with children
  - whether employed by the school full time or part time (and hours worked if part time), and
  - whether resident at the school.
- a personnel file for each member of staff containing a minimum of:
  - their letter of application and any application forms completed
  - their curriculum vitae and employment history where this has been requested by the school
  - evidence that appropriate checks have been carried out
  - a copy of their contract of employment
  - copies of or evidence of qualifications
  - any references the school has obtained
  - interview notes where taken
  - details of any disciplinary action taken against them.
- details of any other person living or working at the school's premises
- an accident log of all accidents occurring to children while they are looked after by the school, or to staff or visitors at the school
- menus (as served) for the past year

- duty rosters recording the identities of the staff and other persons who actually worked at the school or with children from the school, by both day and night

- a diary of events occurring at the school, including the names of visitors to the school and the reasons for their visits (the latter may be kept in a separate visitors' book if wished).

19.3 The above records (other than menus) are retained for at least 5 years from the date of the last entry.

Contact

OUTCOME

In accordance with their wishes children are able and encouraged to maintain contact with their parents and families while living away from home at school.

STANDARD 20

20.1 Subject to their wishes, children are positively encouraged and enabled by the school to maintain contact with their parents and other family members (unless there are welfare concerns) while living at school.

20.2 Staff contact parents regarding any welfare concerns relating to children at the school.

20.3 Any restrictions on contact with parents, family members or other persons imposed by a court, local authority personnel authorised to do so or a parent are implemented by the school.

20.4 The school itself only imposes restrictions or monitoring of a child's telephone, written or electronic contacts with parents or family members where there is clear evidence of a significant risk of harm to the child from such contacts, and a record is kept of any such restrictions and the reasons for them.

20.5 Children are able to meet parents or other visitors at school in comfortable and private surroundings.

20.6 Staff receive training to develop skills to work with children and their families.

Preparation for leaving care

OUTCOME

Children about to leave care are prepared for the transition into independent living.

STANDARD 21

21.1 **Where a pupil is in care and will be leaving care on leaving the school, the school agrees with the young person's responsible authority what contribution it should make to implementing any Pathway or other plan for the pupil before the pupil leaves school. These arrangements are in line with that young person's needs, and the school implements its contribution where feasible from at least a year before the pupil is expected to leave care or move to independent living[5]. The school works with any Personal Advisor for the child.**

21.2 The daily life of the school provides opportunities for all children in the school, appropriate to the age and needs of each child, for the development of knowledge and skills needed by the child for their likely future living arrangements.

Support to individual children

OUTCOME

Children receive individual support when they need it.

STANDARD 22

22.1 **All children are given individualised support in line with their needs and wishes, and children identified as having particular support needs, or particular problems, receive help, guidance and support when needed or requested.**

22.2 The school actively promotes the involvement of all children in social groups, counters isolation of individuals by others, and supports those children who for any reason do not readily fit in to the resident group.

22.3 Support is provided for any child for whom English is not their first language (or who use alternative methods of communication), enabling them to communicate their needs, wishes and concerns, and to communicate with staff and other children within the school.

22.4 Children are able to contact any member of staff with personal or welfare concerns, not only their designated key workers.

---

5   Such a plan may include making arrangements and preparing for further or higher education in employment, independent accommodation, managing personal finances and benefits, health care, securing needed advice and supports, establishing social contacts, hobbies and leisure activities, and daily living tasks such as shopping and cooking.

22.5   The school provides professional services where necessary to help children develop individual identity in relation to their gender, religious, racial, cultural or linguistic background, their disability and/or SEN or sexual orientation.

22.6   Support and advice is provided to any child in the school who is, or has been, involved in abuse or prostitution, whether as a victim of abuse or in abusing others, and the child is involved in the planning of any such programme of support.

22.7   Children undergoing times of personal stress (including homesickness) are supported within the school.

22.8   The school identifies to each child at least one person, independent of the school and/or the child's placing authority, whom they may contact directly about personal problems or concerns at the school. The person identified must be able to communicate with the child either directly or through an independent third party. Such a person may for example be an advocate, a children's rights officer, an adult family member, personal advisor, befriender, visitor on behalf of an organisation carrying on the school, independent visitor, counsellor or mentor. If appointed by the school, such independent persons have been subject to the same vetting checks as are required under these Standards for staff of the school. They are required to follow the school's child protection procedures where they become aware of allegations or suspicions of abuse or other significant harm to any child from the school.

22.9   Children who require specialist external services (eg for recreation, health, education or legal representation/advice) receive those services in practice. Staff cooperate in implementing any programmes associated with specialist services such as speech and language therapy or physiotherapy programmes.

22.10   The school ensures the provision of individually appropriate personal, health, social and sex education for each resident child, including children with disabilities.

22.11   The school ensures that where applicable, relevant personal, educational and health information concerning each child is passed on to that child's subsequent placement.

22.12   Any specific therapeutic[6] technique is only used with any child at the school if specified in the child's placement plan and if agreed by the child's placing authority in the case of a child placed by a local or health authority or the child's parent where applicable. Additionally the safe and effective use of the technique is known to be supported by evidence. It is carried out only by, on the directions of, or under the supervision of a member of staff or other practitioner holding a current recognised qualification in the therapy concerned, whose qualification the school has verified as valid and appropriate directly with the awarding body or relevant register. Any such member of staff using such a technique is subject to supervision in using the technique by a person outside the school and not responsible for the school, who is qualified and experienced in the therapy concerned.

22.13   Children are given appropriate support following any traumatic incident.

---

6   A therapeutic technique is any technique intended to treat or relieve a physical, social, emotional, behavioural, psychological or cognitive problem of a child, the application of which requires skills or knowledge beyond the skills or knowledge normally expected of a parent, teacher or care worker.

7

Premises

Location, design, size

OUTCOME

Children live in well designed and pleasant premises, providing sufficient space and facilities to meet their needs.

STANDARD 23

23.1 **The school is located, designed and of a size and layout that is in keeping with its Statement of Purpose. It serves the needs of the children and provides the sort of environment most helpful to each child's development, and is sufficient for the number of children.**

23.2 Where the school accommodates children with disabilities, suitable aids and adaptations and any special furniture or equipment required are provided to enable them to live as normal a life as possible. Particular attention is paid to the following:

- accommodation ensures that children with disabilities have all necessary access to all parts of the building and site they need to use

- handrails and other mobility aids are sited where appropriate

- there are not excessive numbers of, nor problematically steep, slippery, narrow or unprotected ramps in buildings or grounds

- any lifts and stairs are adapted and safe for all users

- if children have visual impairments, colours and lighting are chosen to offset the loss of vision

- if children have hearing impairments, an induction loop or similar amplification system, necessary telephone and television adaptations and noise insulation are provided

- safe storage of equipment and wheelchairs, with proper arrangements for recharging wheelchair batteries

- enabling children to pass through doors without assistance where possible – eg by installing doors which can be pushed open in either direction from a wheelchair, with a safety vision panel where appropriate, at a suitable height for wheelchair users

- sufficient space and appropriate layout of premises, equipment and furniture to enable children with mobility problems or using wheelchairs or other mobility aids to move reasonably freely around the school.

23.3 There are no outstanding requirements or recommendations (other than any being implemented within the timescale recommended by the relevant authority) relating to the school from any of the following bodies:

- planning authority

- building control authority

- fire service

- environmental health authority.

23.4 Where a school has resident disabled children an occupational therapist has assessed the premises and their recommendations have been adhered to.

23.5 The school's premises are not also used for functions or activities that compromise or have an adverse effect on the care or privacy of children in the school.

23.6 Effective precautions, acceptable to children and staff, are taken to ensure the security of the school from access by unauthorised persons, without compromising or having an adverse effect on the care of children in the school.

23.7 Auditory, electronic or visual monitoring systems are not used inside the school unless:

- currently specifically required within the placement plan for any individual child concerned or,

- specifically approved by that child's placing authority or parent or,

- specifically required by a court,

and provided in the school's statement of purpose. Such equipment is solely for the purpose of safeguarding and promoting the welfare of the child or of other children in the school, and with the full knowledge, subject to the age and understanding of that child and any other children affected.

23.8 Physical restrictions on normal movement within boarding accommodation (eg stairgates, high handles on doors) are only used in relation to a child where the restriction has been agreed within their placement plan (and care plan in the case of a child looked after by a local authority), and are only used where necessary to satisfactorily safeguard and promote that child's welfare. Such restrictions for one child do not impose similar restrictions on other children.

23.9 The school maintains appropriate links with the local community to the school and where appropriate promotes positive links between the children and the community.

Accommodation

OUTCOME

Children live in accommodation which is appropriately decorated, furnished and maintained to a high standard, providing adequate facilities for their use.

STANDARD 24

24.1 The school provides adequate good quality and well maintained accommodation for boarding pupils, which is consistent with their needs.

24.2 The school's residential accommodation and facilities for pupils out of class time are appropriately decorated and furnished to an acceptable standard which creates a pleasant and as far as practicable, a homely residential environment, appropriate to the age, culture and ethnic background of the children being accommodated and the community.

24.3 The interior and exterior of the school is maintained in a good state of structural and decorative repair. Damage to the premises and furniture (including vandalism and graffiti) is repaired promptly. Grounds and play areas and fixed play equipment are well maintained and safe.

24.4 During term time, residential accommodation for pupils is reserved for the exclusive use of the pupils for whom it is designated, with other pupils only having access by reasonable invitation of pupils living in that building or unit.

24.5 Children do not sleep in bedrooms, dormitories, or partitioned areas of larger rooms[7], and as far as possible children are given the option of a single room. There are no more than four children in a bedroom and at no time are there odd numbers of children sharing a bedroom. Any request by a child to change bedrooms is considered and agreed if feasible. Bedrooms or dormitories have:

- sufficient and suitable beds and bedding,
- carpet or other appropriate floor covering,
- a window providing adequate natural light by day,
- curtains or other window coverings,
- seating,
- lighting sufficient to read by and
- heating.

Each child has:

- storage for clothes and
- lockable or otherwise safe storage for personal possessions.

---

7 Where (e.g. in converted listed buildings) children sleep in larger rooms, these should be partitioned by built partitions or partitioning furniture to achieve separate sleeping areas each for no more than 5 children. (DN: This may need amending – whatever is agreed with DfES about no.s in a room)

24.6 Children do not share bedrooms or dormitories with adults, with children of significantly different age[8], or with children of the opposite gender.

24.7 All children are able and encouraged to personalise their bedrooms or dormitories within reason.

24.8 Children's bedrooms or dormitories are not consistently considered overcrowded or too small by either children or staff.[9]

24.9 Telephones, textphones and other similar communication systems provided for the exclusive use of children in the school offer acceptable levels of privacy for personal calls, and are maintained in working order, any damage or breakdown being promptly repaired. The number and location of these ensures accessibility for all residential pupils, and is sufficient to avoid significant queuing at peak times. Pupils with disabilities are enabled to use them in private as far as is possible.

24.10 There are facilities for children to study outside teaching time, which are quiet, with sufficient seating and desk or table space, adequately lit, with adequate storage for books and study materials, and available when needed for study purposes.

24.11 There are facilities for children to pursue personal hobbies at the school, with sufficient and secure storage for safekeeping of materials.

24.12 Children are given opportunities to have a say in the general décor, furnishings and upkeep of the school if they wish.

24.13 There are facilities for laundering bedding and clothes, and domestic style facilities for children to learn to wash, dry and iron their own clothes if they wish and are able to do so and if this is appropriate in relation to their placement or leaving care plan. Bedding is kept acceptably clean. Where necessary schools provide sluicing and washing facilities for soiled laundry.

24.14 The lighting, heating and ventilation of all parts of the school is satisfactory and fully meets the needs of the children.

24.15 There are rooms in which children can meet privately with visitors and space for private activities, play and recreation.

24.16 Visiting arrangements do not cause other children to be excluded from carrying on routine activities.

24.17 Staff have designated sleep-in rooms located close to children's bedrooms to respond to children's night time needs. Where more than one staff member sleeps in there are separate sleeping in rooms.

---

8 As a general guide, 'significantly different' age should be interpreted as over two years' age difference, or being in non-adjacent year groups, unless there is a good reason in particular circumstances to apply a different interpretation.

9 Where it is necessary to refer to physical space standards in borderline assessments of rooms in planning accommodation, or where there is a dispute over room sizes, the guidelines in the School Premises Regulations 1999 should be followed. These require single bedrooms to have at least 6m^2 of usable floor space, and for rooms for more than one child to have at least 1.6 m^2 plus 4.2 m^2 per child of usable floor space.

24.18 Where necessary because of children's disabilities or other needs, an effective emergency call system is provided with sufficient and appropriately located call points readily accessible to children in emergency (eg pull cords that can be reached after falling). The system is operational and effective in summoning prompt staff assistance.

24.19 Where needed by children, the school provides sufficient and appropriate equipment such as lifts, hoists and wheelchairs, and such equipment is regularly serviced. Staff using such equipment have been appropriately trained.

Bathroom and lavatories

OUTCOME

Children are able to carry out their personal care in privacy and with dignity.

STANDARD 25

25.1 The school has sufficient baths, showers and toilets, all of good standard and suitable to meet the needs of the children. The school has appropriate changing and washing facilities for incontinent children where necessary.

25.2 There is at least one toilet for four children accommodated, close to and readily accessible from sleeping accommodation, with adjacent hand washing and drying provision. In boys' residential units, urinals may be provided instead of no more than two thirds of the required number of WCs where appropriate. If pupils have ensuite WC provision, one WC not in ensuite provision should be provided per four pupils who do not have their own ensuite facilities.

25.3 Both baths and showers are available for children's use, and there is a minimum of one bath or shower for every seven children accommodated. There is a higher ratio when required by children's needs. Normally the majority of the required provision should be showers.

25.4 Hot and cold water supplies are adequate for normal levels of use by children and staff.

25.5 Bathrooms, showers and toilets are sited and designed to take account of the children's needs for privacy, dignity and safety, and are readily accessible from sleeping and recreational areas of the school. Doors can be locked but staff are able to open them from the outside in case of emergency; such doors are not easily opened from the outside by other children. Showers not in individual rooms are provided in individual cubicles or are fully individually curtained for privacy. Unless requiring assistance or supervision, children can bath, shower and use the toilet in private. Any child who needs assistance or supervision with bathing, showering or toileting should has provided in a manner that maximises privacy and dignity.

25.6 Bathrooms and toilets are accessible to disabled children in accordance with the school's Statement of Purpose.

25.7   Staff and adult visitors use separate toilet and bathroom or shower facilities to those used by children.

Health, safety and security

OUTCOME

Children live in schools that provide physical safety and security.

STANDARD 26

26.1   Positive steps are taken to keep children, staff and visitors safe from risk from fire and other hazards, in accordance with Health & Safety and Fire legislation and guidance.

26.2   There are no significant unnecessary hazards to health and safety apparent in the school or grounds. Gas installations are inspected at least annually. Electrical installations and equipment are checked at least every three years. Boilers are maintained annually.

26.3   Risk assessments are carried out, recorded in writing and regularly reviewed. Such risk assessments are carried out with regard to:

- the school's premises and grounds (including windows which present a risk to children or offer intruder access; safe car parking etc),

- children's known and likely activities (both permitted and illicit),

- particular risks arising from the disabilities of any child at the school,

- risks arising from children not able to appreciate hazards for themselves,

- potential risks to children from public access to children at the school or during activities or outings,

- where applicable the impact of emergency admissions to the school for both the admitted child and the existing child group.

26.4   The Head of the school or other senior member of staff regularly reviews the implementation and effectiveness of action identified as a result of risk assessments carried out.

26.5   Children and staff know the emergency evacuation procedures for the school, including those for use at night, in case of fire, and confirm that they have regularly practised such evacuation through fire drills.

26.6   Fire drills, and the regular testing of emergency lighting, fire alarms and fire fighting equipment, are performed in accordance with Fire Regulations and any supplementary guidance received from the Fire Authority. Any deficiency identified from drills or tests is noted, and action taken as necessary to remedy the deficiency.

26.7   The school has consulted the local Fire Authority where further significant extension, change of use or alteration has been made to the premises. The recommendations of the Fire Authority have been implemented within any timescales set by that authority.

26.8   Hot water temperature at taps accessible to vulnerable children does not exceed 43 degrees C. Radiator and hot water pipes accessible to vulnerable children do not have a surface temperature exceeding 43 degrees C. Lack of vulnerability is determined by written risk assessment.

26.9   Where the school uses medical devices and equipment, or equipment for disabled children (eg hoists, lifts, wheelchairs), the school has arrangements to receive and respond to relevant hazard and other warning notices from the Medical Devices Agency and to service regularly and maintain equipment in good and safe order.

26.10   Any animals kept at the school and accessible to children are appropriately looked after to maintain reasonable hygiene, and do not present a significant risk to children's health and safety (eg through risk of injuring children, or triggering allergies in particular children).

8

Staffing

Child protection – Vetting of staff and visitors

OUTCOME

There are careful selection and vetting of all staff, volunteers, and monitoring of visitors to the school to prevent children being exposed to potential abusers.

STANDARD 27

27.1 Recruitment of all staff (including ancillary staff and those employed on a contractual/sessional basis) and volunteers who work with children in the school[10] includes checks through the Criminal Records Bureau checking system (at Standard or Enhanced level as appropriate to their role in the school), with a satisfactory outcome. There is a satisfactory recruitment process recorded in writing.[11]

27.2 The school's system for recruiting staff (including ancillary staff, contract/sessional staff and volunteers) who will work with children in the school includes all of the following elements, which should be verifiable in recruitment records held at the school:

i   check of identity against an official document such as a passport or birth certificate

ii   Criminal Records Bureau check at the highest available level

iii   at least two written references, including the most recent employer, with a reference request letter that specifically asks all referees to state any known reason why the person should not be employed to work with children and that there should be no material mis-statement or omission relevant to the suitability of the applicant

iv   direct contact by the school with each referee to verify the reference

v   interview, with a written record of the outcome

vi   check on proof of relevant qualifications

---

10   Definition of working with children is as used by the Criminal Justice and Court Services Act 2000.

11   The Government has issued guidance on staff recruitment in *Working Together to Safeguard Children*, Guidance for schools is also available in the 'Boarding Briefing' series published by the Boarding Schools' Association.

vii   requirement that applicants supply a full employment history, stating that any previous employer may be approached by the school

viii   contact by the school, where possible, with each previous employer involving work with children or vulnerable adults to check the reasons the employment ended

ix   explanation of any gaps in CV, with a written record by the school that explanations for any gaps have been sought and are satisfactory.

27.3   For all adults who after April 2002 begin to live on the same premises as children/students (for example adult members of staff households) but are not employed by the school, there is a verifiable Criminal Records Bureau check completed at the standard level.

27.4   Appointment of 'gap' student staff includes every element of the above recruitment checking system that is possible (even if the student concerned is already known to the school or to a trusted school abroad or is recruited through an agency).

27.5   Where Criminal Records Bureau checks or equivalent are not available for 'gap' student staff, the school obtains a 'certificate of good conduct' or equivalent from the relevant authorities of the student's home country where such facilities are available.[12]

27.6   Offers of appointment to staff and others subject to the above recruitment checks are made subject to satisfactory completion of Criminal Records checks and satisfactory references if not all yet received.

27.7   Staff members (and others) subject to the requirements set out in 7.2 do not begin work (or residence) at the school until satisfactory completion of all checks and receipt of references. Exceptionally, a member of staff may begin work if some references/checks are outstanding, but all Criminal Records Bureau checks or equivalent must have been completed. In such cases, there must be evidence that every effort has been made to chase the checks and references, and the person must be supervised so that they do not have substantial unsupervised access to children at the school.

27.8   Criminal Records Bureau checks and references are included in the recruitment process for any Guardians arranged by the school, and all adults living or working in lodgings arranged by the school, with a satisfactory outcome received and recorded in writing by the school before any child is placed in the school.

27.9   The school *either* has Criminal Records Bureau checks or equivalent on agency staff or has evidence that the agency has carried out the necessary checks within the last 12 months. The school has taken all reasonably practicable steps to carry out Criminal Records Bureau checks or to satisfy themselves such checks have been carried out on taxi drivers booked by the school to drive children at the school unaccompanied by staff.

---

12   Guidance on Cerificates of Good Conduct and equivalents is given in DfES Circular 9/93 *Protection of Children: Disclosure of Criminal Background of those with Access to Children.*

Adequacy of staffing establishment

OUTCOME

Children are looked after by staff who understand their needs and are able to meet them consistently.

STANDARD 28

28.1 The school is staffed at all times of the day and night, at or above the minimum level specified under standard 28.2. Records of staff actually working in the school demonstrate achievement of this staffing level.

28.2 The school's staffing policy ensures that the level of staffing is adequate to meet the school's Statement of Purpose[13]. The school's staffing policy states:

- the number of care staff required to be on duty by day (which may include different required numbers for different circumstances), in the evenings and during weekends

- the number of care staff required to be on duty by night, and whether they are required to be waking or sleeping in

- the arrangements for managing the staff on duty group by day and night

- the arrangements for calling senior staff support if required.

28.3 The school's staffing levels by day and night are appropriate to fulfil the school's Statement of Purpose, to meet the needs of the children, and to provide levels of supervision for children that are safe for children, staff and members of the public.

28.4 There is a continuity of staff such that children's relationships are not overly disrupted. No more than half the staff on duty at any one time by day or night at the school are to be from an external agency and no member of staff from an external agency is to be alone on duty at night in the school.

28.5 The school increases the number of staff looking after children above the minimum required by the staffing policy where children's needs or other circumstances require this.

28.6 In all cases where children under 15 are resident a minimum of two staff must be on duty between 7 am and 11 pm each day children are resident. Where a single member of staff is on waking or sleeping in duty at night (11 pm to 7am) a risk assessment has been carried out and recorded in writing (eg in a daily log), identifying any likely risks to children, staff and members of the public, and this has demonstrated that there is no unacceptable level of risk from such an arrangement.

---

13 Special schools are staffed in line with guidance produced by DfES in Circular 11/90.

28.7 There is at least one adult in charge of each identifiable group of children, within or outside the school, with the means to call for immediate back up from at least one other member of staff if necessary. Children are able to identify the member(s) of staff who are on duty and responsible for them, and how they can be contacted if necessary.

28.8 Where children under 15 are resident at least one member of staff is present, sleeping in or on waking night duty, in each residential unit of the school at night, responsible for the children in that unit and contactable by them at any time of the night. Where children of 15 or over are resident any decision regarding the need for staff presence at night has been subject to a written risk assessment.

28.9 Where only one member of staff is with a child or group of children either in the school or with children away from the school, that staff member has the means to call for back up from another member of staff if necessary

28.10 The school has clear and appropriate arrangements for the supervision, and where necessary, escorting, children on journeys arranged by the school, which are sufficient to meet the children's needs and provide reasonable supervision and control during the journey

28.11 Staff cover arrangements for staff sickness and absence enable the level of staffing set out in the school's staffing policy to be maintained.

28.12 The staff group in day to day contact with children includes staff of both genders. In rare cases where the school's Statement of Purpose makes it explicit that the school uses staff of one gender only, clear guidance is provided and implemented on how children are enabled to maintain relationships with members of the opposite gender to the staff group.

28.13 Staff have a written record of which children and adults are sleeping in each residential unit each night and that record is easily accessible.

Training and staff development

OUTCOME

Children are looked after by staff who are trained to meet their needs.

STANDARD 29

29.1 Staff receive training and development opportunities that equip them with the skills required to meet the needs of the children and the purpose of the school.

29.2 The school has an induction training programme for all newly appointed care and ancillary staff (including any agency, temporary, volunteer, and student staff), which includes guidance on child protection. New staff are supervised, clear about accountability and reporting lines, and procedures to be followed in relation to emergencies, health and safety, child protection and notification of incidents.

29.3   All staff of the school have access to continuing and where applicable, post qualifying training in child care.

29.4   Subject to the needs of individual staff there are programmes of training available which address the issues detailed in Appendix 2.

29.5   Each member of staff has a personal development plan.

29.6   Staff working in any capacity with children at the school have received training appropriate to their role within the school about the needs of children accommodated at the school. Such training has addressed the appropriate response to and management of the children and in any special means of communication used by one or more children at the school.

Staff supervision and support

OUTCOME

Children are looked after by staff who are themselves supported and guided in safeguarding and promoting the children's welfare.

STANDARD 30

30.1   All staff, including domestic staff and the Head of the school, are properly accountable and supported.

30.2   All staff and others working in the school (including the teachers, care staff, temporary staff and ancillary staff) receive at least one and a half hours one to one supervision from a senior member of staff each half term. New staff receive one to one supervision at least fortnightly during the first two terms of their employment. Agency staff and those employed infrequently to cover staff absences must receive one to one supervision no less frequently than once in every half-term they work more than ten shifts (or days) at the school.

30.3   Records are kept of agreed action required, by both the supervisor and the staff member following supervision meetings.

30.4   Supervision addresses issues such as the staff member's role, their work with any child for whom the staff member is key worker, their responses to and methods of working with children, the staff member's work in fulfilling the placement plans for individual children and their degree of personal involvement, feelings, concerns and stress. Supervision will also include staff development and training, the setting and maintenance of standards, feedback on performance, as well as guidance on current and new tasks.

30.5   Suitable arrangements exist for professional supervision of the Head of the school.

30.6   All staff have their performance individually and formally appraised annually by their line manager (for teachers this will normally be part of Performance Management and does not require a separate process). The employee's personal file contains a record of the appraisal (or Performance Management notes) showing the level of performance achieved, targets for the coming year, and the agreed training needs to be met within the following year as part of the individual's Personal Development Plan.

30.7   Staff are provided with written guidance on procedure and policy that is kept up to date, is accessible, and where applicable address the issues detailed in Appendix 3.

30.8   There are clear lines of accountability from the Head of the school to the governors or other person or body responsible for carrying on the school (except when the Head is also the proprietor). All staff know to whom they are accountable.

30.9   All staff have received written job descriptions and person specifications related to the school's current Statement of Purpose which state clearly the duties currently expected of them and their accountability line. Job descriptions are subject to periodic review.

30.10   Rotas are organised to allow appropriate groups of staff to meet together at least monthly. Staff meetings include discussion of both the school's work in caring for individual children and the management of the current child group, together with review of the school's practices. Ancillary staff attend at least part of these meetings on a regular basis. Meetings have an agenda and are minuted. Schools should have full staff meetings at least termly.

30.11   Where the school's Statement of Purpose or declared ethos or method of working requires external specialist guidance and support to staff, this is made available either on an individual basis or through staff meetings.

30.12   Staff do not smoke while with pupils, nor consume alcohol while on duty (including during breaks in their working day).

9 Organisation and management

Staffing arrangements

OUTCOME

Children receive the care and services they need from competent staff.

STANDARD 31

31.1 The school is organised, managed and staffed in a manner that delivers the best possible child care.

31.2 By 2005, the Head of Care (or equivalent post holder) has at least three year's experience at a senior level in a child care setting and a professional qualification relevant to working with children, which must be either NVQ level 4 or the Diploma in Social Work or another qualification with demonstrates competencies at the level of the NVQ.

31.3 Staff members rostered to be in charge of the school and other staff at particular times (eg as leaders of care staff shifts) have substantial relevant experience of working in the school or a similar school.

31.4 By 2005, a minimum ratio of 80% of care staff have completed their Level 3 in the Caring for Children and Young People NVQ or have qualifications which demonstrate the same competencies as the NVQ. New care staff engaged from January 2004 hold such qualifications or begin working towards them within three months of joining the school.

31.5 Staff rotas have time scheduled to ensure that the following occur without compromising overall care of children:

- staff supervision
- staff meetings
- handover sessions
- completing records
- planning and carrying out care programmes
- spending time interacting with individual children

- annual reviews of statements

- individual education plan reviews

- transition reviews.

31.6 Staff working hours are consistent with the requirements of the school's Statement of Purpose and meet the requirements of the Working Time Directive.

31.7 Children are not given responsibility over other children in the school, nor given responsibilities to compensate for any lack of staff in the school. Children who are given responsibility for specific tasks in the school are sufficiently supervised by staff to ensure that they fulfil their roles appropriately, without abuse of the role (eg to bully others).

31.8 Following any allegation or suspicion of abuse of a child by a staff member or other person working at the school, a decision on whether or not to send home the member of staff, pending investigation and as a neutral action in relation to the outcome of the investigation or any subsequent decision making, has been made with first consideration being given to the interests of children in the school.

31.9 The school has planned responses to a range of forseeable crises (eg outbreaks of illness, fires, serious allegations or complaints, significant accidents, staff shortages, and control problems within or outside the school), and any major incidents or crises since the last inspection have been satisfactorily managed.

31.10 The school provides information to the parents of each child resident in the school (unless to do so is impracticable or would be contrary to the welfare needs of that child) which summarises the school's child protection, anti-bullying, disciplinary, complaints, health and pastoral policies and practice. Additionally it provides the contact telephone numbers and addresses of the local social services authority should parents wish to make direct contact in relation to child protection and of the National Care Standards Commission for other issues.

31.11 If applicable under relevant Regulations, the school ensures that its care staff are registered with the General Social Care Council.

Business management and internal monitoring

OUTCOME

Children and staff enjoy the stability of efficiently run schools.

STANDARD 32

32.1 **The National Care Standards Commission is informed within 24 hours if a receiver, liquidator or trustee in bankruptcy becomes responsible for the school. Such persons on becoming responsible for the school have ensured that the school continues to be managed on a day to day basis by a Head who meets the recruitment and qualification requirements for a Head under these Standards. Such a temporary Head must make sure that the operation of the school meets the requirements of these Standards in relation to the day to day care of the children accommodated at the school.**

32.2 The Head or senior members of staff, delegated by the Head to do so, monitor and sign the following records as noted, to identify any patterns or issues requiring action, and takes any required follow up or consequential action:

Half termly

- Each child's placement or other plan
- Duty rosters as actually worked
- Menus
- Accidents and injuries
- Medication, treatment and first aid at the school
- Allegations or suspicions of abuse and their outcomes
- Complaints and their outcomes
- Visitors to the school and to children in the school
- Notifications of incidents to the inspecting body
- Absence of children without authority
- Sanctions applied
- Use of physical intervention.

Termly

- Staff recruitment records and conduct of required checks for any newly recruited staff
- Risk assessments and subsequent action
- Deposit and issue of money and valuables given for safe keeping
- Fire drills and tests of alarms, emergency lighting and fire equipment
- Minutes of staff meetings.

Annually

- Staff appraisals and Performance Management.

32.3 Action has been taken if necessary in relation to any concentration, trend or pattern in recorded issues or events (eg relating to particular places, individuals or times).

32.4 The Head of the school once each year carries out, and records in writing, a review of the operation and resourcing of the school's welfare provision for boarding pupils, in relation to its Statement of Purpose, its staffing policy, the placement plans for individual children, and an internal assessment of its compliance with these Standards, and submits that report to the governing body or other proprietor of the school. Where appropriate such a report may be incorporated within a review of the whole school. Items identified as requiring attention are incorporated into the school's development plan.

32.5 The school has considered and recorded the reasons for any high incidence of police involvement with children from the school, or high staff turnover. Any consequential action necessary is carried out.

Monitoring on behalf of the person carrying on the school

OUTCOME

The governing body, trustees, local authority, proprietor or other responsible body monitors the welfare of the children in the school.

Standard 33

33.1 The governing body, trustees, local authority, proprietor or other responsible body receive a written report on the conduct of the school from a person visiting the school on their behalf half termly.

33.2 The governing body, trustees, partnership, or organisation responsible for carrying on the school arrange for one of their number or a representative who does not work at, or directly manage, the school, to visit the school once every half term and complete a written report on the conduct of the school. Where the school has an individual proprietor, that person may carry out such visits personally if they are not also the Head.

33.3 The majority of visits counted as meeting the above requirement are carried out unannounced. They include:

- checks on the school's records of attendance, complaints, sanctions, and use of physical interventions,

- assessment of the physical condition of the building, furniture and equipment of the school, and

- opportunities for any child or member of staff who wishes to meet the visitor (in private if they wish).

33.4 Written reports of all above visits are provided to the Head of the school within two weeks of the visit. Where the school is carried on by a governing body, organisation, or partnership reports are also provided to each member of that body (or the appropriate committee of that body), within two weeks and as written by the visitor without amendment or summary.

33.5 Reports of all above visits are made available to inspectors at the school, and action is taken, and recorded when taken, by the school on recommendations or issues of concern raised in such reports.

33.6 Copies of any inspection reports by the National Care Standards Commission are made available by the school to all members of staff, to children resident at the school, to parents, and on request sent to placing authorities of existing children or those considering placing a child.

Appendices

School procedures for responding to allegations or suspicions of abuse

1. A requirement for referral within 24 hours (in writing or with written confirmation of telephoned referral) of allegations or suspicions of abuse, or other actual or likely significant harm to a child, to the local social services department, rather than investigation by the school;

2. A requirement for joint consideration between the school and the local social services department of subsequent actions, including continuing protection of children in the light of the allegation or suspicion, and when and how to inform any person who is the subject of the allegation or suspicion, and the parents of each child involved;

3. Notification of any allegation or suspicion of abuse, and of the initiation and outcome of any child protection enquiries (under section 47 of the Children Act 1989) involving the school, to any placing authorities of the child(ren) involved;

4. Prompt notification of the initiation and outcome of any child protection enquiries involving the school, to the National Care Standards Commission;

5. Consideration of measures that may be necessary to protect individual children following an allegation or suspicion of abuse being made;

6. The requirement that staff or others working at the school and receiving an allegation of abuse, or suspecting abuse, should avoid asking leading questions or giving inappropriate guarantees of confidentiality;

7. A requirement to report to the police any evidence known of children becoming involved in prostitution, or of unauthorised persons picking children up, contacting children in the school, or observed trying to make contact with children outside the school;

8. A requirement for written records to be made and kept of any allegations of suspicions of abuse, and of actions taken;

9. Instructions for staff on action to be taken if an allegation or suspicion of abuse becomes known to them;

10. Ensuring that both staff and children are provided with information on how they can directly contact the National Care Standards Commission to raise any concerns they have about practices in the school which put children at risk of abuse or serious harm;

11. the requirement upon all staff and others working at the school (including agency staff) to report to the appropriate body any concerns they may have about practices in the school, or the behaviour of colleagues, which they consider likely to put children at risk of abuse or other serious harm;

12. a guarantee that the procedures can be invoked in ways that do not prejudice any whistleblower's own position and prospects if they have reported an allegation or concern in good faith;

13. The procedures make children aware that confidentiality cannot always be guaranteed.

Nothing in this standard removes the duty of schools to inform and work within DfES requirements.

Programmes of training for staff

1.   Child development;

2.   Residential child care skills and team working;

3.   Specific child care approaches and skills appropriate to the school's purpose and function;

4.   Exercising appropriate positive means of control over children in the interests of their own welfare and the protection of others;

5.   Permitted and prohibited sanctions;

6.   Use of physical intervention;

7.   Child protection;

8.   Issues of race, ethnicity, religion and culture;

9.   Dealing with sexuality, sex education and relationships;

10.   Health education relevant to growing children including diet and nutrition;

11.   The implications of HIV and AIDS when looking after children;

12.   Communicating with children, including those with disabilities;

13.   Health and safety at work, including lifting and handling and fire precautions;

14.   Food hygiene;

15.   First Aid and safety with medicines;

16.   The Children Act 1989, these Standards and other related legislation, government guidance and guidance from the National Care Standards Commission;

17.   The provision of purposeful and enjoyable activities outside class time;

18.   Staff supervision;

19.   Interview techniques;

20.   Complaints and representations procedures;

21.   Working with families.

Policies to be accessible to staff with procedures and guidance as appropriate

1. Admission and reception of children;

2. Methods of care and control;

3. Permissible sanctions;

4. Use of physical intervention and dealing with aggression and violence;

5. Case recording and access to records;

6. Planning, using and amending placement or other plans;

7. Equal opportunities;

8. Anti bullying;

9. Log book and diary recording;

10. Confidentiality;

11. Administration of finance (petty cash) and security;

12. Repairs and maintenance;

13. Health and safety including fire precautions and emergency procedures;

14. Countering risks identified through the school's risk assessments;

15. Extent to which all or part of premises may be locked as a security measure;

16. Child protection and responding to allegations or suspicions of abuse;

17. Arrangements for regulating, accompanying and vetting visitors at the school;

18. HIV/AIDS awareness, confidentiality and infection control;

19. Treatment of children who have been abused;

20. Rostering and shift handovers;

21. Sleeping-in, bed-time and night supervision;

22. Physical contact with children and spending one to one time alone with children;

23. Care practices towards children of the opposite sex;

24. The particular care needs of children from minority ethnic groups;

25. Practices within the school to combat racism;

26. Staff disciplinary and grievance procedures;

27. Delegated authority and notifications to senior staff ;

28. Placements;

29. Reviews;

30. Risk taking;

31. Dealing with sexuality and personal relationships;

32. Working with parents/carers;

33. First Aid and administration and storage of medication;

34. The complaints and representations procedures;

35. The smoking policy;

36. The alcohol policy;

37. Gift giving and receiving;

38. 'whistleblowing' by staff.

Glossary

This glossary is designed to help readers in understanding the standards. The definitions do not have any legal weight.

Accommodate (a child)

To provide a child (usually but not always a pupil of the school) with overnight accommodation on school premises, or to arrange the accommodation of a child elsewhere than on school premises (eg in lodgings, a hostel or at the home of a member of staff of the school).

Advocate

A person assisting a child in putting forward their views or making their case on their behalf.

Agency Staff

Staff not employed directly by the school, but provided by an agency which employs them and contracts to provide staff for a specified period to the school.

Ancillary Staff

Staff working at the school in non-teaching and non-care capacities, such as domestic, cleaning, catering, maintenance and grounds staff, and drivers.

Area Child Protection Committee

A group set up to determine the policies and procedures to be followed concerning child protection in a given area.

House

A building, or part of a building, accommodating a defined group of pupils at a school, looked after by one or more designated staff.

Bodily Functions

Using the toilet, personal cleansing, washing, showering, using the bath, dressing, undressing, cleaning teeth, eating and similar everyday personal needs.

Bullying

Note that the Standards require schools to formulate their own definition of bullying, which may reflect issues related to the individual school or its pupils. Generally, bullying in this context would comprise the intentional or perceived causing of pain, distress, anxiety, humiliation or social exclusion to one pupil by one or more other pupils, by physical or verbal means, or through damage or loss of property.

Care Plan

An agreed plan for looking after a child and meeting that child's current and future needs, made by a placing authority under Children Act requirements.

Certificate of Good Conduct

Document available from some countries (sometimes with a different name) confirming that its holder has no outstanding criminal conviction in their country of origin; required where available as part of the recruitment checking process for staff such as gap students recruited from abroad.

Child Protection

Taking reasonable measures to reduce the risk of physical, emotional or sexual abuse, neglect or significant harm of a child, enabling children and staff to report concerns about actual or potential abuse or significant harm, and responding appropriately to allegations, occurrences and suspicions of abuse or significant harm of a child – at school, at home, or outside the school or home.

Child Protection Enquiry

An enquiry into possible significant harm to a child (eg through physical, emotional or sexual abuse, or through neglect), carried out by a local social services authority under section 47 of the Children Act 1989. May include police investigations or investigation by the NSPCC.

Child Protection Plan

A plan identifying a strategy and actions to be taken by (possibly) a number of agencies and individuals to protect a child at risk of significant harm. Likely to follow a child protection enquiry.

Contract Staff

Staff not employed directly by the school, but by a contractor who carries out work in the school under a contract with the school; eg cleaning, catering, building, driving or maintenance staff of an outside contractor working in or for the school.

Criminal Records Bureau

A national organisation conducting police checks to enable an assessment to be made (eg by a school) on the suitability of a person to work with children. Different levels of check are available for different levels of regular contact and supervisory responsibility for children.

Fire Drill

A trial triggering of a fire alarm and practice of the plan to evacuate children from the building concerned to a safe assembly point, identifying any issues requiring attention to improve the speed and efficiency of such evacuation.

First Aider

A person holding an up to date qualification in administering first aid, from a recognised body, and designated to provide first aid to pupils if required.

Free Time

Time outside teaching, prep and organised activity time, which pupils can decide for themselves how to spend (within reason), either choosing between available optional activities, or choosing to socialise or spend time alone.

Gap Student

A person working as a junior member of staff of a school in the period immediately after leaving their own secondary education (often for a year before entering higher education), often from overseas.

Head

The person in charge of a school, who may be titled its Head Teacher, Headmaster, Headmistress, Principal, Manager or an equivalent title.

High Risk Activities

Activities for pupils which present significant or unusual hazards to pupil safety or welfare, requiring risk assessment and positive safety measures, but which are a reasonable concomitant of a worthwhile activity.

Household Medication

Medicines suitable for children (such as appropriate analgesics) which can be bought 'over the counter' without prescription.

Idiosyncratic Punishments

Punishments which are not approved in the school's disciplinary policy, but are used by individuals against children.

Independent Listener

A person appointed by the school, but not otherwise on the staff of the school, as someone pupils may contact for external support and advice over personal problems or concerns at the school.

Induction

Initial training or guidance given at the start of involvement in living at a school – guidance (eg from an experienced pupil) for a new pupil on arrival at the school; initial training on the school's residential and care policies and practice for a new member of staff.

Intimate Care

Physical assistance or supervision for a child which involves seeing, touching or other contact with the child's normally clothed body, because of the child's disability or care needs – eg assistance with toileting, washing, dressing or undressing, or administration of medication involving these.

Job Description

A written, agreed and up to date statement of the main tasks and responsibilities of a staff member's job within the school, including overall definition of their role and the person to whom they are accountable.

Key Worker

A member of the school staff with particular responsibility for the welfare, guidance and support of an individual child.

Legal Guardians

Persons other than a child's natural parents who have statutory parental responsibility under the Children Act for the child. Does not include the 'educational guardians' arranged by some parents and some schools to befriend or accommodate children, eg in school holidays; these have no legal status or statutory parental responsibility.

Lodgings

Accommodation arranged by the school for a pupil outside school premises (eg in a family home, in a student flat or with a landlord).

National Governing Body (for an activity)

The national organisation or association, or where more than one, the recognised leading organisation or association, which establishes qualifications for instruction and supervision of a sport or activity, together with guidance on its safe practice.

Non-Prescription Medication

Medicines suitable for children (such as appropriate analgesics) which can be bought 'over the counter' without prescription.

Nurse

A person with a current registration and qualification to practice as a nurse in the UK.

Parent

A mother or a father and anyone else with parental responsibility.

Personal Care

Provision of individual help to a child, including help with bodily functions and intimate care.

Personal Development Plan

An agreed plan defining the training and support needs, planned means of meeting these, and the work related goals of a member of staff.

Placement

The agreement for a child to attend and live at a particular place – eg the school.

Placement Plan

An agreed plan defining how a child is to be looked after on a day to day basis at the school, including meeting the child's needs and responding to the child's difficulties, which is consistent with both the school's overall Statement of Purpose and the overall Care Plan for the child concerned made by their Placing Authority.

Placing Authority

A local social services or education authority or health authority or voluntary organisation which has arranged for the child to attend and reside at the school; the authority which is responsible for making and monitoring that arrangement, rather than necessarily the sole funding authority for the placement.

Positive Reinforcement

Positive consequences for acceptable behaviour or progress of a child, intended to recognise and encourage such behaviour or progress.

Representations

Complaints, concerns or major issues raised with the school or a placing authority by or on behalf of a child about their care or welfare.

Restitution

A disciplinary measure or punishment in which the child is expected to 'make good' or repay an individual or the school for the consequences of unacceptable actions or damage they have done. An alternative to more artificial sanctions, but should always be reasonable, feasible and proportional to the actions concerned.

Physical Intervention

Use of reasonable physical intervention or force to prevent injury or serious damage to property.

Risk Assessment

The process of identifying hazards to safety or welfare of children, estimating their seriousness and likelihood, and identifying reasonable measures to minimise unnecessary hazards, recorded in writing as the basis for an action plan and decision making to reduce unnecessary hazards to children.

Sanctions

Any negative consequences applied for unacceptable behaviour – eg punishments, loss of privileges or duties to be carried out.

School Development Plan

Agreed plan for the operation, premises, financing and any changes for the school as a whole.

Significant Harm

Any physical, sexual, or emotional harm, neglect, accident or injury which is sufficiently serious adversely to affect the child's expected or normal development, progress and enjoyment of life.

Sleeping In

Staff responsible for pupils within a house or unit at night, but asleep within the house or unit and 'on call' to be woken if needed.

Staff Recruitment Checks

Clearances with the Criminal Records Bureau, Department of Health and Department for Education and Skills required to ensure that candidates to have regular contact with children are not known to be unsuitable persons for such contact.

Statement of Purpose

A document which defines the objectives and welfare provision of the school, and covers those issues defined in the National Minimum Standards.

Statutory Review

A review of a child's care and care plan carried out as required by Regulations under the Children Act by the child's placing authority.

Stock (of medication)

Medication kept for general use for any child needing it, rather than prescribed medication kept only for the child for whom it was prescribed.

Substantial Unsupervised Access (to pupils)

Where an adult has regular or prolonged contact with pupils, or access to pupils' accommodation which provides opportunity for such contact, without another adult responsible for the welfare and supervision of the pupils being present.

Supervision of children

Effective management and care of children. This does not mean that a member of staff is at all times present, but involves the child knowing who is responsible for them, how that person can be contacted; and involves the member of staff being present and nearby as and when necessary to ensure that they can take effective responsibility for the welfare of the child.

Unit

A building, or part of a building, accommodating a defined group of pupils at a school, looked after by one or more designated staff.

Waking (night duty)

Where a member of staff on duty at night in the school (or in an individual residential house or unit) remains awake and fully available and supervising the premises and children at all times throughout their night duty period, as opposed to sleeping in or staying in a sleeping in room and only woken if needed.

Welfare

Meeting each individual child's reasonable physical, security, personal, emotional, and spiritual needs, providing support and guidance as needed, and enabling the child's normal development for the future and fulfillment in the present, taking into account the child's age, characteristics and wishes.

'Whistleblower'

A person who in good faith reports significant concerns, allegations or suspicions of circumstances, situations or the behaviour of others which is likely to put a child's safety or welfare at risk.

Inspection Regulations

STATUTORY INSTRUMENTS

2002 No. 552

CHILDREN AND YOUNG PERSONS, ENGLAND

The National Care Standards Commission (Inspection of Schools and Colleges) Regulations 2002

Made - - - - -	*7th March 2002*
Laid before Parliament -	*11th March 2002*
Coming into force - -	*1st April 2002*

The Secretary of State, in exercise of the powers conferred upon him by sections 87(6) and 104(4) of the Children Act 1989(a), and of all other powers enabling him in that behalf, hereby makes the following Regulations:—

Citation, commencement and extent

1.—(1) These Regulations may be cited as the National Care Standards Commission (Inspection of Schools and Colleges) Regulations 2002, and shall come into force on 1st April 2002.

(2) These Regulations extend to England only(b).

Interpretation

2.—(1) In these Regulations—

"the 1989 Act" means the Children Act 1989;

"authorised person" means a person authorised by the appropriate authority(c) to exercise the power of entry conferred by section 87(5) of the 1989 Act; and

"relevant school or college" means a school or college to which section 87(1) of the 1989 Act applies.

(2) In these Regulations, a reference in a regulation to a numbered paragraph is to the paragraph in that regulation bearing that number.

Inspection of premises

3.—(1) An authorised person may inspect any premises, or any part of any premises, which are, or are to be, the premises of a relevant school or college.

(a) 1989 c. 41, Section 87 of the 1989 Act is amended by sections 105 and 116 of, and paragraphs 14(1) and (21) of Schedule 4 to, the Care Standards Act 2000 (c. 14). See section 105(1) of the 1989 Act for the definition of "prescribed".

(b) The functions of the Secretary of State are, in relation to Wales, transferred to the National Assembly for Wales. See Article 2 of, and the entry for the 1989 Act in Schedule 1 to, the National Assembly for Wales (Transfer of Functions) Order 1999 (S.I. 1999/672), and section 120(2) of the Care Standards Act 2000.

(c) The appropriate authority is, in relation to England, the National Care Standards Commission (see section 87(10) of the 1989 Act).

(2) An authorised person may carry out such examination into the state and management of the premises inspected under paragraph (1) as he considers necessary for the purposes of the inspection.

(3) An inspection under paragraph (1) may take place without notice to the relevant person(**a**).

Inspection of records

4.—(1) An authorised person may inspect any record of a relevant school or college which is relevant to the discharge of the Commission's duty under section 87(3) of the 1989 Act.

(2) The power in paragraph (1) includes power to require the relevant person to produce any records, wherever kept, for inspection on the premises.

(3) In this regulation, a reference to a record includes a record which is kept by means of a computer.

Inspection of children

5.—(1) Subject to the provisions of this regulation, an authorised person may, for the purpose of enabling the Commission to discharge its duty under section 87(3) of the 1989 Act, carry out an inspection of children who are provided with accommodation by a relevant school or college.

(2) An inspection may include a physical examination of a child if the authorised person considers it necessary, and provided that—
- (a) he is a registered medical practitioner or a registered nurse;
- (b) he has reasonable cause to believe that the welfare of the child in question is not being adequately safeguarded or promoted by the relevant person; and
- (c) the child consents to the examination, or is incapable of giving his consent.

(3) An examination under paragraph (2) shall take place in private.

(4) Subject to paragraph (5), an authorised person may interview in private, or solicit written or verbal expressions of opinion from any child or group of children who consent to be interviewed or to express their views, as the case may be.

(5) An authorised person may not interview any individual child in private unless—
- (a) the child concerned has expressly asked to be interviewed alone and in private; or
- (b) the authorised person considers on reasonable grounds that such an interview is necessary to enable the Commission to discharge its duty under section 87(3) of the 1989 Act.

(6) No inspection may be carried out under this regulation in respect of—
- (a) any child of a member of staff of a relevant school or college; or
- (b) any other child living with such a member of staff as a member of his household,

Unless the child is also a pupil or student of the school or college.

Inspection–general

6. An authorised person may in carrying out any inspection under these Regulations—
- (a) require any person to afford him such facilities and assistance with respect to matters within that person's control as are necessary to enable the authorised person to exercise his powers under these Regulations; and
- (b) take such photographs, measurements and recordings as he considers necessary to enable him to exercise his powers.

(**a**) See section 87(11) and (12) of the 1989 Act for the meaning of "relevant person".

[2]

Revocation

7. The Inspection of Premises, Children and Records (Independent Schools) Regulations 1991(**a**) are revoked.

Signed by authority of the Secretary of State for Health

Jacqui Smith
Minister of State,
Department of Health

7th March 2002

(**a**) S.I. 1991/975.

(This note is not part of the Regulations)

These Regulations make provision relating to the inspection of schools and colleges providing accommodation for children. Section 87(5) of the Children Act 1989 (as amended by the Care Standards Act 2000), confers power on a person authorised by the National Care Standards Commission to enter the premises of a school or college accommodating children, in order to determine whether the welfare of the children is being adequately safeguarded and promoted. A person so authorised may inspect the premises of the school or college, its records, and the children accommodated there, as provided for by these Regulations.